Presented to:

Never Forget The Difference You've Made

Made in United States
Orlando, FL
23 June 2022

19081803R00061